COUNTRY 🌎 PROFILES

ISRAEL

BY AMY RECHNER

BELLWETHER MEDIA • MINNEAPOLIS, MN

Blastoff! Discovery launches
a new mission: reading to learn.
Filled with facts and features, each
book offers you an exciting new
world to explore!

This edition first published in 2018 by Bellwether Media, Inc.

No part of this publication may be reproduced in whole or in part
without written permission of the publisher.
For information regarding permission, write to Bellwether Media, Inc.,
Attention: Permissions Department,
5357 Penn Avenue South, Minneapolis, MN 55419.

Library of Congress Cataloging-in-Publication Data

Names: Rechner, Amy, author.
Title: Israel / by Amy Rechner.
Description: Minneapolis, MN : Bellwether Media, Inc., 2018. |
Series: Blastoff! Discovery: Country Profiles | Includes bibliographical
references and index.
Identifiers: LCCN 2017031934 (print) | LCCN 2017033222 (ebook)
| ISBN 9781626177345 (hardcover : alk. paper) | ISBN
    9781681034881 (ebook)
Subjects: LCSH: Israel–Juvenile literature. | Israel–Social life and
    customs–Juvenile literature.
Classification: LCC DS118 (ebook) | LCC DS118 .R43 2018 (print) |
DDC 956.94–dc23
LC record available at https://lccn.loc.gov/2017031934

Editor: Paige V. Polinsky   Designer: Brittany McIntosh

Printed in the United States of America, North Mankato, MN.

TABLE OF CONTENTS

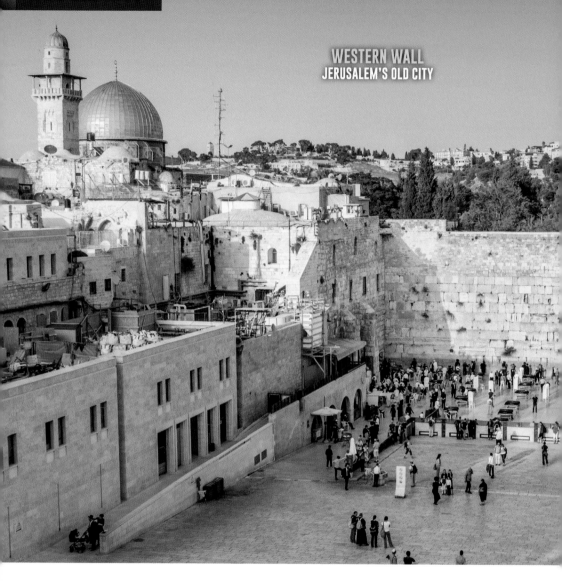

THE OLD CITY

WESTERN WALL
JERUSALEM'S OLD CITY

A family passes through Jaffa Gate into Jerusalem's Old City. They first explore the Armenian Quarter, ducking into shops to admire bright pottery. In the Jewish Quarter, they join a crowd at the Western Wall. Locals and visitors slip written prayers into the wall's cracks.

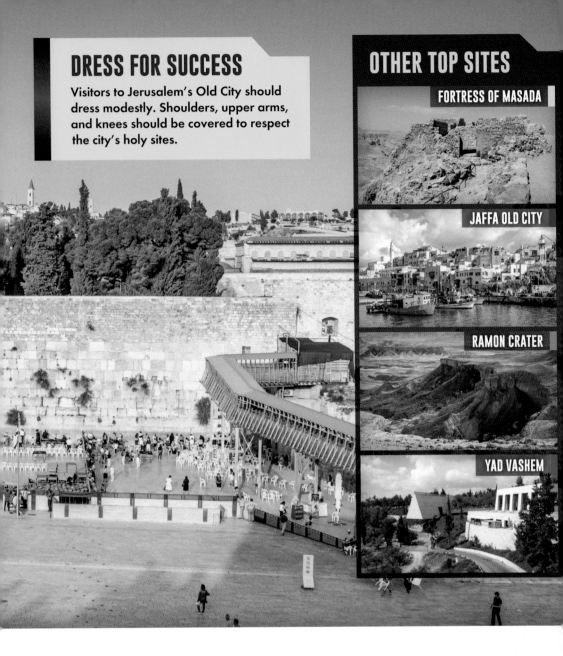

DRESS FOR SUCCESS

Visitors to Jerusalem's Old City should dress modestly. Shoulders, upper arms, and knees should be covered to respect the city's holy sites.

OTHER TOP SITES

FORTRESS OF MASADA

JAFFA OLD CITY

RAMON CRATER

YAD VASHEM

The family crosses stone streets to the Muslim Quarter, where people sell clothes, jewelry, and food from *shuks*, or outdoor markets. Their journey ends in the Christian Quarter at the Church of the Holy Sepulchre. The Old City is a vibrant blend of cultures. This is Israel!

Israel is a long, narrow Asian country just north of Africa. It belongs to a region called the **Middle East**. Israel is bordered by Lebanon to the north and Syria to the northeast. Jordan and the **West Bank** line Israel's eastern side. The Dead Sea is part of this border. To the south, Israel meets the northern tip of the Red Sea. Egypt lies to the southwest. The Mediterranean Sea borders Israel's western coast. The **Gaza Strip** is tucked between Egypt and Israel's coast.

Israel covers 8,019 square miles (20,770 square kilometers). It is slightly larger than the state of New Jersey. Jerusalem, the capital of Israel, lies in the center of the country.

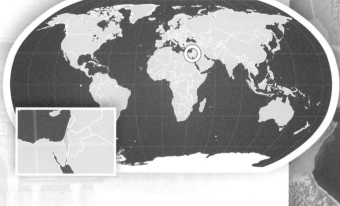

LEBANON

SYRIA

MEDITERRANEAN
SEA

HAIFA

WEST
BANK

JERUSALEM

GAZA
STRIP

TEL AVIV

BEERSHEBA

DEAD
SEA

ISRAEL

JORDAN

EGYPT

JUST A KID

Israel is a young country, only founded in 1948. The land it sits on was formerly called Palestine.

RED
SEA

A mountain range covers northern Israel. It includes Mount Meron, Israel's highest peak at 3,963 feet (1,208 meters). **Plains** of **fertile** farmland stretch south of the mountains toward the western sea. The Jordan **Rift** Valley slices through Israel's eastern countryside. The Jordan River flows south through this valley and empties to the Dead Sea. The Negev Desert spreads over southern Israel.

MT. MERON

JORDAN RIVER

= NEGEV DESERT
= JORDAN RIFT VALLEY

THE GREAT RIFT

The Jordan Rift Valley belongs to a natural trench that runs about 4,000 miles (6,437 kilometers) long.

MOUNT MERON

JERUSALEM
Average seasonal highs and lows

JANUARY
HIGH: 53 °F (12 °C)
LOW: 39 °F (4 °C)

APRIL
HIGH: 70 °F (21 °C)
LOW: 49 °F (9 °C)

JULY
HIGH: 84 °F (29 °C)
LOW: 63 °F (17 °C)

OCTOBER
HIGH: 77 °F (25 °C)
LOW: 57 °F (14 °C)

°F = degrees Fahrenheit
°C = degrees Celsius

Israel's climate is **temperate** in the north and **arid** in the south. Summers are hot and dry. Winters are mild and humid, especially along the coast. Though uncommon, snow sometimes falls in Jerusalem and the northern mountains.

9

Israel's **diverse** landscape attracts wildlife of all types. Gazelles move gracefully through fields of wildflowers. Jackals and wild boars roam through mountain forests. Vultures swoop down from the cliffs above in search of prey.

The Mediterranean coast attracts birds like storks, herons, and egrets. Dusky grouper fish explore the shorelines of the Mediterranean Sea. In the Negev Desert, Arabian oryx gather around rock pools. Arabian wolves and wildcats hunt small rodents in the cool moonlight.

DORCAS GAZELLE

GRAY HERON

DUSKY GROUPER

ARABIAN WOLF

GRIFFON VULTURE

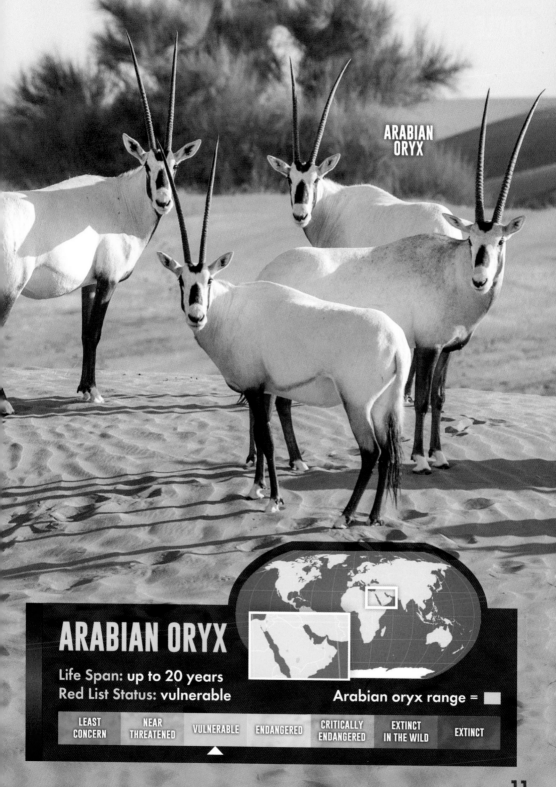

ARABIAN
ORYX

ARABIAN ORYX

Life Span: up to 20 years
Red List Status: vulnerable

Arabian oryx range = ☐

LEAST CONCERN	NEAR THREATENED	VULNERABLE	ENDANGERED	CRITICALLY ENDANGERED	EXTINCT IN THE WILD	EXTINCT

Israel's population is a **complex** blend of cultures.
The country was founded as a homeland where Jewish
immigrants could practice their faith freely. Many of
Israel's 8 million people are Jewish. Their official language
is Hebrew. Many speak English, too.

A smaller number of Israelis are Arab. Many Arab families lived in the area before Israel became a country. Most are Muslim, although many are Christian. They speak Arabic. Because of a long history of conflict, the Jews and Arabs often keep their worlds separate.

FAMOUS FACE
Name: Gal Gadot
Birthday: April 30, 1985
Hometown: Rosh Ha'ayin, Israel
Famous for: Winner of Miss Israel 2004 and action star who plays Wonder Woman in the DC superhero movies

SPEAK HEBREW
The Hebrew language has its own alphabet. However, Hebrew words can be written with the English alphabet so you can read them.

ENGLISH	HEBREW	HOW TO SAY IT
hello	shalom	shah-LOHM
goodbye	shalom	shah-LOHM
please	bevakasha	beh-vah-kah-SHAH
thank you	toda	toh-DAH
yes	ken	kehn
no	loh	low

JERUSALEM

Most Israelis live in apartments in cities like Tel Aviv or Haifa. Many people may live in one building, and neighbors are quick to chat or lend a hand. An Israeli family often has two working parents and more than two children. Israeli children are very independent. They are trusted to explore the community on their own. Kids walk to school with their friends, or they take a bus or train.

TEL AVIV

DAY OF REST

Every Friday at sunset, Israel shuts down for *Shabbat*, the Jewish day of rest. Stores close and public buses and trains stop running. Shabbat ends at sundown on Saturday.

KIBBUTZ

Rural families might live in communities called *kibbutzim*. On a *kibbutz*, several families live and work together. They share the labor, costs, and earnings.

HIJABS

Israeli clothing reflects the country's blend of cultures.
Many Jews wear knit skullcaps called *kippahs*. **Orthodox**
Jews dress in black pants and button-up shirts as well.
Muslim women wear headscarves called *hijabs*. Most
Israelis wear Western clothes, such as jeans and T-shirts.

Israelis are very informal. They enjoy having friends over for large meals. Close friends and family may be greeted with a hug or a kiss on the cheek. However, Orthodox Jews and many Muslims avoid contact with the opposite sex.

YOUNG ADULTS

When Jewish children turn 12 or 13, they have a ceremony called a *bat* or *bar mitzvah*. After a special religious service, they celebrate the end of childhood with a party.

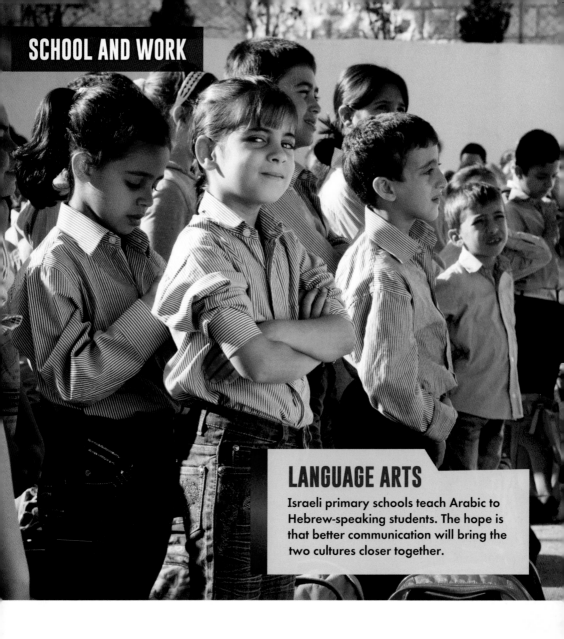

LANGUAGE ARTS

Israeli primary schools teach Arabic to Hebrew-speaking students. The hope is that better communication will bring the two cultures closer together.

Israeli children begin school at age 5. They must attend until age 18. Students can choose from public or private schools. Many teach Hebrew and Jewish studies. Others focus on Arabic and Arab culture. After high school, Jewish students serve in the military for two or three years. They can then begin careers or go to college.

Few Israeli workers are farmers. Many more work in **manufacturing**. They make high-tech communication and medical devices. Most Israeli workers have **service jobs**. They work in areas such as education, **tourism**, and banking.

JEWELRY FACTORY WORKER

SOLDIERS

MATKOT

Israel's sunny shores lure sunbathers, sailors, and surfers. *Matkot*, a popular game similar to paddleball, was invented on Tel Aviv's beaches. People of all ages play tennis, basketball, and soccer. They also cheer for professional teams. Every four years, Israel hosts the Maccabiah Games, an **international** Jewish sporting event like the Olympics. Around 10,000 athletes from 80 countries participated in the 2017 Games.

MUDDY WATERS

The Dead Sea offers Israelis a natural spa. They can float atop the salty waters and smear themselves with mud known for its health benefits. It is most popular with tourists!

Israelis spend time visiting with friends in cafés or shopping together at shuks. Many also enjoy watching TV shows and listening to live music. Public sing-alongs are not uncommon!

SHUK

HAMSA

This ancient good luck charm is used for protection in Muslim and Jewish homes as well as in artwork and jewelry.

What You Need:
- construction paper
- pen or pencil
- scissors
- 1 piece of cardboard
- aluminum foil
- permanent markers, black and blue
- white paint pen
- string or yarn

Instructions:
1. Fold the paper in half the long way.

2. Place your middle finger next to the fold. With fingers close together, trace the middle finger, pointer finger, thumb, and hand. Cut out the hand outline and unfold the paper.

3. Trace the shape onto the cardboard and cut it out.

4. Cover the cardboard with foil, shiny side out. Smooth flat.

5. Use the pen or pencil to outline a large eye in the center of the palm. Paint it white. While it dries, decorate the rest of the hamsa in marker.

6. Draw a black dot in the eye. Add a ring of blue around it.

7. Punch a hole near the base of the palm. Run the string through the hole and knot the ends. Hang up the hamsa to ward off bad luck.

FALAFEL

SPEEDY SNACKS

Israel's most popular fast food is *falafel*, small, deep-fried balls of ground chickpeas. Chickpeas are also the main ingredient in hummus, a popular dip.

Israel grows enough fruit and vegetables to feed the whole country. Local dishes are full of garlic, lemon, olives, and other fresh flavors. Breakfast might include eggs cooked with peppers and tomatoes. Olives, cheeses, and smoked fish are also common. A main meal of meat or fish is served at midday.

Dinner is lighter. One popular dish is an eggplant spread called *baba ghanoush*. This might be served with yogurt, tahini, and pita bread. A salad of chopped tomatoes, onions, cucumbers, and peppers appear at many meals. Shabbat dinners feature chicken soup and *challah*, **traditional** Jewish egg bread.

BABA GHANOUSH

CHALLAH

KADOREI SHOKOLAD (CHOCOLATE BALLS) RECIPE

These sweets are an early childhood memory for many Israelis. No cooking necessary!

Ingredients:
about 30 butter cookies
3/4 cup sugar
5 tablespoons cocoa powder
1/2 teaspoon cinnamon
1/3 cup plus 2 tablespoons milk
1 teaspoon vanilla
7 tablespoons butter or margarine, softened
small bowl of sprinkles or powdered sugar

Steps:
1. Seal the cookies in a gallon-sized plastic bag. Smash them with a rolling pin until they are fine crumbs.

2. Pour the crumbs into a large bowl. Add sugar, cocoa, and cinnamon. Mix well. Add vanilla, butter, and milk, and stir until the batter forms. Add a little more milk if needed.

3. Take a large spoonful of batter and roll it to form a ball. Coat it in sprinkles or powdered sugar and put it on a tray. Repeat until batter is gone. Chill balls for a little while for best results.

CELEBRATIONS

Most of Israel's national celebrations are Jewish holidays. Businesses and schools close to observe holy days such as Passover in the spring. During *Yom Kippur*, Jews **fast** and pray for the new year. Festive holidays like *Purim* and *Simchat Torah* bring costumes, carnivals, and parades to the streets. Every holiday features special treats to eat.

Each spring, people celebrate Israel Independence Day. Israelis of all faiths enjoy film, music, and food festivals all year long. That is the joyous nature of Israel!

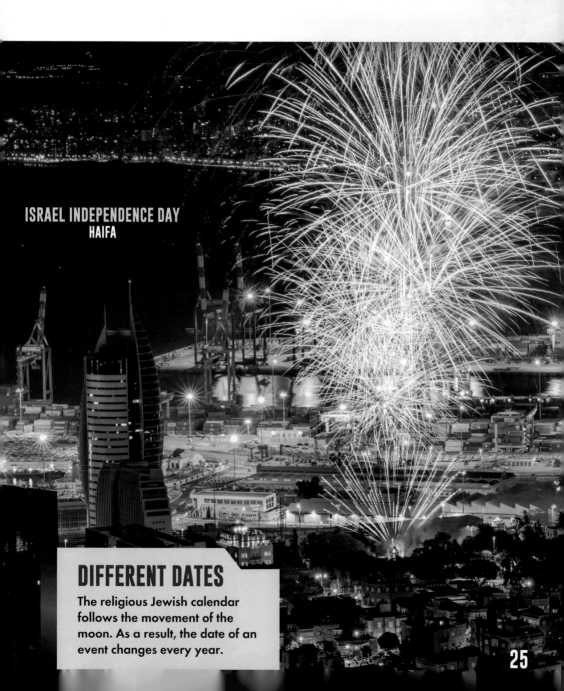

ISRAEL INDEPENDENCE DAY
HAIFA

DIFFERENT DATES
The religious Jewish calendar follows the movement of the moon. As a result, the date of an event changes every year.

1882–1903
Almost 35,000 Eastern European Jews move to Palestine in a wave called the First Aliyah

1945
World War II ends, leaving Jewish survivors to seek refuge in Palestine

1918
World War I ends and Great Britain claims the area called Palestine, hoping for Jews and Arabs to share the land

638
Arabs conquer Jerusalem and the surrounding land, called Palestine

1967
During the Six-Day War, Israel takes the Gaza Strip from Egypt and the West Bank region from Jordan and Syria

1948
Israel declares its independence as a Jewish state and begins fighting in the first Arab-Israeli War, which it wins the following year

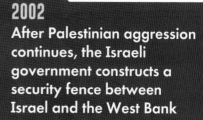

2002
After Palestinian aggression continues, the Israeli government constructs a security fence between Israel and the West Bank

1973
Israel begins fighting Egypt and Syria in the Yom Kippur War, which lasts until 1979

2015
Prime Minister Benjamin Netanyahu is re-elected for a fourth term

Official Name: State of Israel

Flag of Israel: Israel's flag features a white background with a blue six-pointed star, known as the Star of David. The star, an ancient Jewish symbol, is centered between two horizontal blue lines near the top and bottom edges of the flag. The design is similar to a Jewish prayer shawl.

Area: 8,019 square miles
(20,770 square kilometers)

Capital City: Jerusalem

Important Cities: Tel Aviv, Haifa, Beersheba

Population:
8,299,706 (July 2016)

WHERE PEOPLE LIVE

COUNTRYSIDE
7.7 %

CITY
92.3%

JOBS

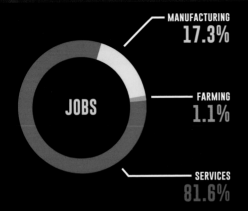

MANUFACTURING
17.3%

FARMING
1.1%

SERVICES
81.6%

Main Exports:

machinery   electronics   chemicals

fuels   diamonds

National Holiday:
Independence Day (date varies)

Main Languages:
Hebrew, Arabic

Form of Government:
parliamentary democracy

Title for Country Leaders:
president, prime minister

RELIGION

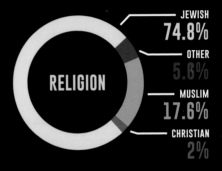

JEWISH
74.8%

OTHER
5.6%

MUSLIM
17.6%

CHRISTIAN
2%

Unit of Money:
new Israeli shekel

GLOSSARY

arid—very dry, with little rainfall

complex—difficult to understand because of having many different parts or ideas

diverse—made up of people or things that are different from one another

fast—to choose not to eat

fertile—able to support growth

Gaza Strip—a small territory along the Mediterranean Sea, neighboring Israel to the southwest; the Gaza Strip is governed by the Palestinian Authority.

immigrants—people who move to a new country

international—related to two or more countries

manufacturing—a field of work in which people use machines to make products

Middle East—a region of southwestern Asia and northern Africa; this region includes Egypt, Lebanon, Iran, Iraq, Israel, Saudi Arabia, Syria, and other nearby countries.

Orthodox—closely following the traditional beliefs of a religion

plains—large areas of flat land

rift—a break in the earth's crust

rural—related to the countryside

service jobs—jobs that perform tasks for people or businesses

temperate—associated with a mild climate that does not have extreme heat or cold

tourism—the business of people traveling to visit other places

traditional—related to customs, ideas, or beliefs handed down from one generation to the next

West Bank—a territory between Israel and the Jordan River; Israel controls part of the West Bank, and the Palestinian Authority controls the other part.

TO LEARN MORE

AT THE LIBRARY

Adler, David A. *Golda Meir: A Strong, Determined Leader.* New York, N.Y.: Puffin Books, 2015.

Owings, Lisa. *Israel.* Minneapolis, Minn.: ABDO Publishing Company, 2013.

Silverman, Elisa. *Understanding Israel Today.* Hockessin, Del.: Mitchell Lane Publishers, 2014.

ON THE WEB

Learning more about Israel is as easy as 1, 2, 3.

1. Go to www.factsurfer.com.

2. Enter "Israel" into the search box.

3. Click the "Surf" button and you will see a list of related web sites.

With factsurfer.com, finding more information is just a click away.

INDEX

The images in this book are reproduced through the courtesy of: Lals Stock, front cover; Olesya Baron, pp. 4-5; Ido Kalish, p. 5 (top); Gerardo C. Lerner, p. 5 (middle top); Valery Shanin, p. 5 (middle bottom); JekL, pp. 5 (bottom), 14; Brittany McIntosh, pp. 6-7, 8 (inset); Design Pics, Inc./ Alamy, p. 8; Hanan Isachar/ Alamy, p. 9; Meunierd, p. 9 (inset); Sergei25, p. 10 (top); Vadim Petrakov, p. 10 (middle top); Sait Ozgur Gedikoglu, p. 10 (middle bottom); Carmine Arienzo, p. 10 (bottom left); C. Paul Fell, p. 10 (bottom right); Juan Martinez, pp. 10-11; Bildagentur Zoonar GmbH/ Alamy, p. 12; D. Free, p. 13 (top); Nir Levy, p. 13 (bottom); Naive/ Alamy, p. 15; Andyman/ Alamy, p. 16; Lucas Vallecillos/ Alamy, p. 17; J. Carillet, p. 18; Fotokon, p. 19 (top); Salvador Aznar, p. 19 (bottom); Verbaska Studio, p. 20 (top); Robert Hoetink, p. 20 (bottom); Alexey Stiop, p. 21 (top); Engin Korkmaz, p. 21 (bottom); Ivoha/ Alamy, p. 22; Vlastimil Kuzel, p. 23 (top); Studio Evasion, p. 23 (middle); Nata Vkusidey, p. 23 (bottom); Itsik Marom/ Alamy, p. 24; Ruslan Kalnitsky, p. 25; Pikiwikisrael, p. 26; Zefart, p. 27 (top); Yakub88, p. 27 (bottom); Fat Jackey, p. 29 (currency, coins).